Deb Duncan & Todd Duncan
New York Times bestselling author

5 STARS

WORKBOOK

Building High Ratings and
High Trust in the Digital Age

simple truths
small books. **BIG IMPACT.**

Photo Credits
Front cover: Yganko/Shutterstock, zaniman/Shutterstock
Internals: page 1, Yganko/Shutterstock, zaniman/Shutterstock

Published by Simple Truths, an imprint of Sourcebooks, Inc.
P.O. Box 4410, Naperville, Illinois 60567–4410
(630) 961-3900
Fax: (630) 961-2168
www.sourcebooks.com

Printed and bound in the United States of America.

VP 10 9 8 7 6 5 4 3 2

High-Trust, High-Tech Tips

What Can Change the Future of Selling?

★ **Get Real.** See the consumer as a real person, not just a transaction or sale. The new mandate is connection. The deeper the connection, the higher the conversion and the ratings.

★ **Reviews Rule.** Accept the fact that social media and technology give your customers a megaphone when it comes to relaying good or bad experiences.

★ **Balanced Technology.** Automation and innovative communication can be extremely helpful in creating a successful consumer experience. However, they can also zap the productivity of sales and service personnel who spend more time reacting to immediate opportunities than adding to the bottom line.

★ **Be Intentionally Purposeful.** Strive to find a noble purpose as it relates to your product or service. Have your customers experienced that impact? Focusing on social causes boosts return on investment dramatically.

★ **Reboot Follow-Up.** Reinvigorate the most important fundamental of business. The tighter the follow-up, the more likely the sale. Without follow-up, there is no follow-through.

In Your Own Business...

How you can create deeper connections with your customers?

_____

_____

_____

_____

What can you do to increase the effectiveness of your follow-up?

_____

_____

_____

_____

What Won't Change in the Future of Selling?

★ **Trust Trumps Tech.** It always has; it always will. The challenge is to make sure tech accelerates, supports, and grows trust. No company can hide behind tech and expect trust to flourish. Trust is the catalyst that ignites business, and trust must remain at the forefront of all endeavors if ratings are to be as high as possible.

★ **Focused Selection Leads to More Opportunity.** Now more than ever, careful selection and deselection strategies will be necessary to filter through the waves of sales leads being generated. The digital world has simplified lead aggregation, but it has not increased effectiveness in selecting those leads. It's not the number of leads that matter, it's the number of sales and purchases. It's a productivity game, not a numbers game. Simplification is centric to the quality of leads rather than the quantity of leads. Conversion must be the bottom line of all bottom lines.

★ **Communication and Connection Accelerate Conversion and Referrals.** Conversion does not increase unless connection goes deep. If you don't connect, you won't convert. All messaging, all conversations, all communications must impact the customer emotionally and experientially to win the sale and 5 Stars.

★ **Proven Solutions Will Earn Higher Prices.** This requires focus, skills with automation tools, and flat-line management. Speed of trust will require exceptional listening skills over the delivery of factual information. A combined effort on social graces, interpersonal relationships, positive attitudes, fun, collaboration, and leadership will win the sale.

In Your Own Business...

How do you ensure that the aggregation of leads focuses on quality and not quantity?

_____

_____

_____

_____

How can you increase the conversion rate for your business?

_____

_____

_____

_____

High-Trust, High-Tech Tips

★ **Create the Level of Total Trust a Customer Experiences.** It's a philosophy that must be part of your company culture and core values—it must be the heartbeat of your brand, and each person in your company must commit to creating it.

★ **Put the Customer at the Center of the Transaction.** The emphasis is not on the sale. The 5-Star Company knows that the sale is the by-product of the perceived value and socially proved value.

★ **Deliver Uncommon Levels of Service at Every Stage of the Buying Experience.** It's about blowing the customer's mind and simultaneously blowing the doors off business as usual. This must be relentlessly pursued.

★ **Fall in Love with Your Customers.** If you don't love them, they *will* leave you. The number one strategy to accelerate retention

and incite repeat and referral business is showcasing how much your company cares for and loves the customers that make your business a business.

★ **High Tech Supports High Trust, Not the Other Way Around.** High tech is suspicious when trust does not exist first. A study by research and consulting firm YouGov showed that as many as 50 percent of U.S. consumers do not trust what they see, read, or hear in advertisements. Show how and why your company helps the consumer first, and then show the products' qualities second.

★ **High Tech Does Not Create Connection Unless High Trust Exists.** On their own, email, web messages, advertisements, and texts are viewed as low-trust advertising methods and rarely advance the customer experience.

★ **High Tech Must Positively, Emotionally, and Memorably Impact the Customer at Every Point of the Buying Experience.** High tech must be informative, valuable, engaging, consistent but not overbearing, and yes, even fun.

★ **High Tech Is Having a Serious Negative Impact on Employee Performance, Creativity, and in Many Cases, Morale.** Thousands of hours or more of employee time are being consumed by technology with no increase in revenue, and, in many cases, technology is creating performance stress that is not healthy for a company if it wants to be fully functional.

In Your Own Business...

How can your company put the customer at the center of each transaction?

_____

_____

_____

How do your customers know you love them?

_____

_____

_____

How can you apply the examples of Blue Hawaiian Helicopters and Nashbar to your own business to create a 5-Star experience for your customers?

_____

_____

_____

Ten Ways You Can Use Technology to Create Trust

Technology has enabled us to accelerate trust with clients. In just a few clicks, we can make customers happier than ever before. Here are some ideas to get you started:

1. Send automated texts thanking the customer.
2. Send automated emails thanking the customer.
3. Request reviews and surveys.

- ⊙ Automated call: Time Warner calls you for a review after an interaction with a service technician.
- ⊙ Text: Bank of America texts you to request your opinion on its location after you visit a branch.
- ⊙ Email: Delta emails you to prompt a review of your flight experience twenty-four hours after you land.
- ⊙ App notification: Fandango sends you a push notification for a survey two hours after you've seen a movie.

4. Comment on and respond to customer social media posts—make sure to balance push marketing with engagement marketing.

5. Entergagement (Entertainment + Engagement)—provide value in a fun and creative way through daily content, apps, videos, contests, sweepstakes, and infographics.

6. Call customers to make sure they are happy after their purchases.

7. Provide lifetime warranties—overdeliver on the promise and remove the risk.

8. Provide frictionless web and mobile payments—Amazon perfected this, as did Fandango, Starbucks, and Uber. Make sure to view as the consumer to nail this.

9. Maintain social responsibility—social media spreads companies' social causes like wildfire.

10. Communicate quickly with customers—be responsive; speed matters.

What customer contact methods will be most effective at your company?

_____

_____

_____

_____

_____

High-Trust, High-Tech Tips

★ The Law of the Iceberg: the truest measure of your success is invisible to your clients.

★ The Law of the Iceberg creates a laser focus for your organization and team.

★ The stickier the customer is to your brand, the faster your brand will grow.

★ Generally, the more purposeful a company is, the higher its ratings will be.

In Your Own Business...

The Law of the Iceberg works in every organization. How can your company become more purposeful at its core to provide more impact with its products and services?

_____

_____

_____

_____

To grow an "Iceberg" culture, answer these eight questions with your team. You will engineer passion and purpose into your organization.

The Law of the Iceberg Checklist

☐ What does your picture of success look like?

_____

_____

_____

☐ Why are you in business?

_____

_____

_____

☐ What do you want your brand to be known for?

_____

_____

_____

☐ How does what you do matter?

_____

_____

_____

☐ Where are you going?

_____

_____

_____

☐ What will guide you?

_____

_____

_____

☐ What difference are you going to make?

_____

_____

_____

☐ How will your customer be transformed?

_____

_____

_____

High-Trust, High-Tech Tips

Productive, engaged employees are more likely to create happy customers, which lead to higher ratings.

5-Star Moves for Taming Technology

- ★ **Batching**: handle all technology-related tasks at predetermined times.

- ★ **The Cone of Silence**: remove yourself from the digital grid to improve results.

- ★ **The 5-Minute Rule**: evaluate whether you were productive the last fifty-five minutes and reset for the next hour.

★ **Jamming**: force productivity on the most important thing you can do over the next hour.

★ **Delegation in the Digital Age**: focus on what you are good at and delegate the rest.

In Your Own Business...

Rate the items below on how much each ambushes time at your company, with 1 taking the most time and 6 taking the least time.

___Email
___Text
___Social Media
___Meetings
___Interruptions
___Emphasis on Multitasking

What could you do to enhance your productivity?

_____

_____

_____

_____

What could the company do to enhance personal productivity?

_____

_____

_____

_____

What changes could be implemented for more effective meetings in your organization?

_____

_____

_____

_____

What other ways could communication be more effective in your organization?

_____

_____

_____

_____

High-Trust, High-Tech Tips

★ If your story is compelling, it imprints on your customers' hearts, brains, and memories.

★ Using video creates a more compelling story.

★ Remember the seven most important elements to great story*selling*.

1. Simple
2. Short
3. Easily repeatable
4. Memorable
5. Emotional
6. Includes a grand promise
7. Compelling

In Your Own Business...

What is the key story you want to tell at your company?

_____

_____

_____

_____

Stories are always better with a hero, a villain, and a goal. The following are some key questions to consider when shaping your story.

HERO:

Why did you launch the company?

_____

_____

What is your grand purpose?

_____

_____

What is the emotion you are trying to tap into?

_____

_____

Why are you committed to and passionate about the opportunity?

_____

_____

VILLAIN:

What problem needed to be solved?

_____

_____

GOAL:

What is your unique factor? How are you different from the pack? What sets you apart? How is your philosophy superior to your competition's?

_____

_____

_____

High-Trust, High-Tech Tips

- ★ Emotionally engage your customers.

- ★ Pull your customers into a relationship with your brand.

- ★ Target your dream clients—those highly influential people who can affect more than one referral, or sometimes thousands.

- ★ Remember the best form of advocacy is word-of-mouth.

- ★ Optimize the customers' experiences *every* time.

- ★ Cultivate your customers for repeat business.

In Your Own Business...

List specific examples of how your customers' experiences are transformed because of your product or service. The more emotional the better.

_____

_____

_____

_____

What questions could your sales team ask to create more of an emotional connection with your customers?

_____

_____

_____

LOVE ZONE NO. 1: ACQUIRING NEW CUSTOMERS

How do you define your dream client?

_____

_____

_____

How can you incentivize customers to spread positive information about your company?

_____

_____

_____

What is your word-of-mouth strategy?

_____

_____

_____

LOVE ZONE NO. 2: OPTIMIZING THE CUSTOMERS' BUYING AND SERVICE EXPERIENCES

How can you avoid a $6,000-Egg situation at your company?

_____

_____

_____

If you fall short, what is your recovery strategy so you don't lose that customer forever?

_____

_____

_____

LOVE ZONE NO. 3: RETAINING AND CULTIVATING CUSTOMERS FOR REPEAT AND REFERRAL BUSINESS

The High-Trust, High-Tech Retention Checklist

- ☐ Are you creating a positive connection with the customer?
- ☐ Do you demonstrate your committed concern for the customer?
- ☐ Do you create an environment for a long-term relationship?
- ☐ Does your product or service truly transform the customer's business and life?

- [ ] Do you ask deep and meaningful questions to keep the customer engaged?
- [ ] Do you have a trustworthy acquisition and retention strategy?
- [ ] Are you constantly delivering real value that creates brand lock-in?
- [ ] Are your reviews 5 Stars more than 90 percent of the time? If not, think about what you need to do differently.
- [ ] Do you leverage your *earned advertising* from your loyalists to help you grow?
- [ ] Are you establishing *trustology*?

High-Trust, High-Tech Tips

- ★ A virtual handshake exists before you even meet your customers.

- ★ Nail the first impression with customers.

- ★ Go big with service.

- ★ Make milestones matter.

- ★ Keep them coming back.

- ★ Nail the last impression.

In Your Own Business...

What improvements can you make to your virtual presence to communicate or story*sell* your company's message?

_____

_____

_____

How can you use technology to create a virtual handshake with your customers?

_____

_____

_____

RATE HOW WELL YOU DO AS A COMPANY IN THE FOLLOWING CATEGORIES:

Nailing the First Impression with Customers

Poor First
Impression

Hit a
Home Run

What steps can you take to improve?

_____

_____

_____

Going Big with Service

☹ |——————|——————|——————| ☺

*Fell Short of
Customer
Expectations*

*Exceeded
Customer
Expectations*

What steps can you take to improve?

_____

_____

_____

Making Milestones Matter

☹ |——————|——————|——————| ☺

*Didn't Recognize
Milestones*

*Recognized
Milestones like
Clockwork*

What steps can you take to improve?

_____

_____

_____

Keeping Them Coming Back

☹ |——————|——————|——————| ☺

Didn't Follow Up

*Made It Easy for
a Second Sale*

What steps can you take to improve?

_____

_____

_____

Nailing the Last Impression

*Didn't Contact
after Transactions*

*Surveyed Regularly
during and after
Transactions*

What steps can you take to improve?

_____

_____

_____

High-Trust, High-Tech Tips

★ If your service is not at *level ten*, you will lose sales, revenue, and if you are not careful, your company or your job.

★ World-class service is not the future! It is here now, and if you are not on board, you will lose!

★ The key to having a successful 5-Star company rests in the Law of the Encore, which states: the greater the performance, the louder the applause.

★ Getting customers to say "wow" is about doing things differently than the rest of the market.

In Your Own Business...

How can you reach *level-ten* service at your company?

_____

_____

_____

How can you create a movement with your product or service like TOMS did?

_____

_____

_____

How else can you "wow" your customers?

_____

_____

_____

High-Trust, High-Tech Tips

★ Advocates are far more valuable than advertisements.

★ The value of a business is in the strength and stickiness of its customers.

★ Connect with your customers' hearts before ever speaking to their heads.

★ To become a "sticky" brand, keep your content simple, attention-getting, emotional, compelling, and consistent. Tell a story.

★ Competition is not for customers' money; it is for their emotions.

In Your Own Business...

HUMANIZE YOUR COMPANY

Creating real, meaningful value for your customers takes some introspection. Here are some questions to begin:

How can you connect at a deeper level with your customers through sales and service?

_____

_____

_____

What questions can you ask to get to know your customers better and connect more meaningfully?

_____

_____

_____

How can you make doing business less painful for your customers?

_____

_____

_____

What do your customers really want, and how can you go beyond that in what your product or service provides?

_____

_____

_____

BUILD VALUE THAT STICKS

How can you change your messaging so that your customers become "stickier" and can't live without you?

_____

_____

_____

MAKE SURE YOUR BRAND HAS EMOTIONAL ATTACHMENT

Review the following questions about your connection with your customers:

How valuable are your current connections?

_____

_____

_____

How frequently do you connect with your customers?

_____

_____

_____

How do you make your customers feel special and loved?

_____

_____

_____

What could you do to create a stronger connection with your customers?

_____

_____

_____

What are the top ten emotional points of value customers experience with your products or services?

1. _____
2. _____
3. _____
4. _____
5. _____
6. _____
7. _____
8. _____
9. _____
10. _____

Does your technology inspire and build trust?

_____

_____

_____

High-Trust, High-Tech Tips

- ★ Different generations want to be sold in different ways.

- ★ Baby Boomers are high touch and prefer personal contact.

- ★ Generation X is digitally engaged. Keep it short and stick with the facts.

- ★ Millennials love the Internet, social media, and mobile marketing. Make your message an emotional story.

In Your Own Business...

Who makes up the majority of your customer base: Baby Boomers, Gen Xers, or Millennials?

_____

What is the most effective way of marketing your product or service to each of the following generations:

Baby Boomers

_____
_____
_____

Gen Xers

_____
_____
_____

Millennials

_____
_____
_____

CLOSING THOUGHTS

We hope *5 Stars* has empowered you with all the tools necessary to become a great leader in selling your business's story and creating success. We believe any professional can achieve success through these strategies—including you! We hope you've enjoyed the experience and growth that *5 Stars* strives to provide.

For more information on *5 Stars* and other Simple Truths and Todd Duncan products, please visit SimpleTruths.com.

ABOUT THE AUTHORS

Deb Duncan is president of American Television Ventures. She has been a pioneer in the direct-response television industry. Starting in college, she was a producer of *Everybody's Money Matters* on the Lifetime Television Network. She has written, produced, and directed more than one hundred direct-response TV programs. She has great insights on how to frame your message and how to get people to respond. Deb is the author of two children's fairy tales, *A Thousand Princes* and *Mrs. Prince*, as well as several screenplays.

For more than twenty years, **Todd Duncan** has earned a transformative reputation worldwide as a top trainer, motivator, and personal coach for business professionals in the sales, mortgage, real estate, and financial services industries. Todd's influence in the peak-performance world impacts more than 250,000 people annually around the globe, and he has personally coached some of the world's top-producing sales professionals.

Todd is the author of sixteen books, including the *New York Times* best-sellers *Time Traps: Proven Strategies for Swamped Salespeople* and *High*

Trust Selling: Make More Money in Less Time with Less Stress. His books are in forty-four languages with more than one million copies in print.

Todd has been featured in the *New York Times*, the *Wall Street Journal*, the *Los Angeles Times*, the *Seattle Times*, *Entrepreneur* magazine, and *SUCCESS* magazine, and on the Success Network, *The Dave Ramsey Show*, and FOX News, among other media outlets.

As leading experts in the field of High Trust Selling™ and service training and development, Deb and Todd provide real solutions to the challenges businesses face in the new world of commerce.

Have Todd and Deb Speak at Your Next Event

To explore having Todd and Deb speak at your next corporate meeting or training, or to inquire about additional services, contact Alicia Barata at alicia.barata@toddduncan.com.